BASEBALL
All-Stars

Players in a league of their own

Kane Miller
A DIVISION OF EDC PUBLISHING

First American Edition 2020
Kane Miller, A Division of EDC Publishing

Copyright © Green Android Ltd 2020

For information contact
Kane Miller, A Division of EDC Publishing
P.O. Box 470663
Tulsa, OK 74147-0663
www.kanemiller.com
www.edcpub.com
www.usbornebooksandmore.com

ISBN 978-1-68464-136-9
Library of Congress Control Number: 2019952966

Please note that every effort has been made to check the accuracy of the information contained
in this book, and to credit the copyright holders correctly. Green Android Ltd apologize for
any unintentional errors or omissions, and would be happy to include revisions to content
and/or acknowledgements in subsequent editions of this book.

Printed in China, August 2020.

Image credits Aaron Judge © Frank Franklin II/AP/Shutterstock, Aaron Nola © Matt Slocum/AP/Shutterstock,
Albert Pujols © Matthew Trommer/Dreamstime.com, Alex Bregman © Eric Christian Smith/AP/Shutterstock,
Andrelton Simmons © Mark J Terrill/AP/Shutterstock, Anthony Rizzo © Matt Marton/AP/Shutterstock, Babe Ruth
© Commons.wikimedia.org/ Irwin, La Broad, & Pudlin/Public Domain, Blake Snell © Chris O'Meara/AP/Shutterstock,
Bryce Harper © Nick Wass/AP/Shutterstock, Carlos Correa ©Commons.wikimedia.org/Keith Allison, Charlie
Blackmon © commons.wikimedia.org/jenniferlinneaphotography, Chris Sale © Elise Amendola/AP/Shutterstock,
Christian Yelich © Morry Gash/AP/Shutterstock, Clayton Kershaw © Commons.wikimedia.org/Arturo Pardavila III,
Cody Bellinger © Sam Gangwer/AP/Shutterstock, Corey Kluber © Colin E Braley/AP/Shutterstock, Corey Seager
© Nick Wass/AP/Shutterstock, Danny Jansen © Julio Cortez/AP/Shutterstock, Eugenio Suarez © Jeff Roberson/AP/
Shutterstock, Francisco Lindor © David Banks/AP/Shutterstock, Freddie Freeman © Patrick Semansky/AP/
Shutterstock, George Springer © Commons.wikimedia.org/ KA Sports Photo/Public Domain, Gerrit Cole © JOHN G
MABANGLO/EPA-EFE/Shutterstock, Giancarlo Stanton © Albert Pena/CSM/ Shutterstock, Greg Maddux © Jerry
Coli/Dreamstime.com, Hank Aaron © Sports Images/Dreamstime.com, J. D. Martinez © Canadian Press/Shutterstock,
J.T. Realmuto © Chris Szagola/CSM/Shutterstock, Jacob DeGrom © John Minchillo/AP/Shutterstock, Javier Baez
© Matt Marton/AP/Shutterstock, Jimmie Foxx © Commons.wikimedia.org/ Harris & Ewing/Public Domain,
Joe Dimaggio © Commons.wikimedia.org/Heritage Auctions/Public Domain, Joey Votto © Ross D Franklin/AP/
Shutterstock, Jose Altuve © Eric Christian Smith/AP/Shutterstock, Jose Ramirez © AP/Shutterstock, Juan Soto
© Eric Gay/AP/Shutterstock, Justin Turner © Julio Cortez/AP/Shutterstock, Justin Verlander © Frank Franklin II/AP/
Shutterstock, Ken Griffey © Jerry Coli | Dreamstime.com, Kris Bryant © Matt Marton/AP/Shutterstock, Lorenzo
Cain © David Zalubowski/AP/Shutterstock, Luis Severino © Brandon Wade/AP/Shutterstock, Marcell Ozuna © Jeff
Roberson/AP/ Shutterstock, Matt Carpenter © Jeff Roberson/AP/Shutterstock, Matt Chapman © Mary Altaffer/AP/
Shutterstock, Matt Olson © David J Phillip/AP/Shutterstock, Max Scherzer © Matt Slocum/AP/Shutterstock, Mickey
Mantle © Commons.wikimedia.org/Heritage Auctions/Public Domain, Mike Trout © Albert Pena/CSM/Shutterstock,
Mitch Haniger ©Kathy Willens/AP/Shutterstock, Mookie Betts ©Phelan M Ebenhack/AP/Shutterstock, Nolan
Arenado © Gregory Bull/AP/Shutterstock, Paul Goldschmidt © Matt Marton/AP/ Shutterstock, Randy Johnson
© Scott Anderson/Dreamstime.com, Ronald Acuna Jr. © John Amis/AP/Shutterstock, Ted Williams © Commons.
wikimedia.org/Heritage Auctions/Public Domain, Trevor Bauer © Rick Scuteri/AP/ Shutterstock, Trevor Story
© David Zalubowski/AP/Shutterstock, Whit Merrifield © Charlie Riedel/AP/Shutterstock, Xander Bogaerts
© Michael Dwyer/AP/Shutterstock.

BASEBALL All-Stars

CONTENTS

TOP 10 ALL-TIME LEGENDS

These are the players who helped make baseball the thrilling spectacle it is today.

1 BABE RUTH

1914 – 1935   1936

Ruth was six feet tall and weighed two hundred pounds. His height and weight made him a heavy hitter – his career home run record (714) stood for over 40 years. But the "Sultan of Swat" was also a fast hitter – he reacted to pitches more quickly than most other batters.

OUTFIELDER PITCHER

2 HANK AARON

1954 – 1976   1982

Aaron's motto was "Always keep swinging." And he did – Aaron was the player who finally broke Babe Ruth's career home run record (755). His batting style earned him the nickname "Hammerin' Hank." The winner of three Gold Glove Awards, Aaron still holds several MLB records.

RIGHT FIELDER

3 TED WILLIAMS

1939 – 1960   1966

Considered by many to be the greatest batter of all time, Williams's career OBP (.482) remains a record, and his SLG (.634) and OPS (1.116) rank second. His strong wrists, thin frame, agility, and batting ease led to the nickname "Splendid Splinter." Williams was the last player to hit .400 or better in a season.

LEFT FIELDER

4 GREG MADDUX

1986 – 2008   2014

Maddux pitched with laser accuracy and total consistency. "The Professor" had more than 300 wins and 3,000 strikeouts, and fewer than 1,000 walks in his career. Thirteen times he threw complete shutouts in under 100 pitches. Maddox was the first pitcher to win the Cy Young Award four seasons in a row.

PITCHER

ALBERT PUJOLS

ONE TO WATCH

Pujols' 656 home runs through the 2019 season rank him sixth in MLB records. He's still playing, so the records of Mays, Rodriguez, Ruth, Aaron, and Bonds are not safe.

★ ★ ★

5 MICKEY MANTLE

1951 – 1968   1974

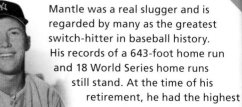

Mantle was a real slugger and is regarded by many as the greatest switch-hitter in baseball history. His records of a 643-foot home run and 18 World Series home runs still stand. At the time of his retirement, he had the highest stolen base percentage in history. "The Mick" played in 12 World Series and won seven!

CENTER FIELDER • FIRST BASEMAN

These players have the records, honors, and awards, but they also gave the game something extra special, setting the field on fire with the best hitting, pitching, and fielding. Some had single, legendary feats, and others slow-burned into brilliance. Who's your choice for best of the best?

6 JOE DIMAGGIO

1936 – 1951　　1955

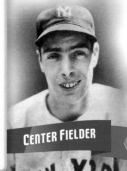

CENTER FIELDER

"Joltin' Joe" played his entire 13-year career for the New York Yankees. He led them to 10 World Series and won nine. He wowed fans with his hitting, fielding, and base running. His 56-game hitting streak in 1941 is a record unlikely to be broken. His two brothers were also Major League center fielders.

GREG MADDUX

RECORD FIELDER

Greg has won the Rawlings Gold Glove Award a record 18 times. He received the award every year from 1990 to 2002, and then from 2004 to 2008.

★ ★ ★

7 KEN GRIFFEY JR.

1989 – 2010　　2016

Nicknamed "The Natural," Griffey made baseball look effortless with his perfectly balanced swing. The son of MLB All-Star Ken Griffey Sr., his 630 home runs sit seventh in MLB records. His easy-going nature, electric smile, and love of the game helped define a new era for baseball's popularity.

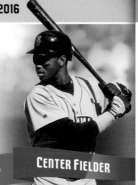

CENTER FIELDER

8 JIMMIE FOXX

1925 – 1945　　1951

Foxx made his MLB debut before the end of his junior year in high school. Nicknamed "The Beast," he hit harder than anyone and was the second player in MLB history to hit more than 500 home runs. Foxx was voted MVP three times, and was the first player to win back-to-back MVP Awards.

RIGHT FIELDER

9 ALBERT PUJOLS

2001 –　　NOT ELIGIBLE YET

As a child, Pujols used limes as balls and a milk carton for a glove. He grew up to become one of the greatest right-handed batters, and "The Machine" is known for the consistency of his swing. Pujols is tied for the most seasons (14) with more than 100 RBIs and is sixth in career home runs (656).

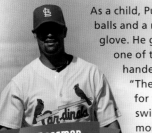

FIRST BASEMAN

10 RANDY JOHNSON

1988 – 2009　　2015

At 6'10", "The Big Unit" used his height to his advantage. Johnson's fastballs and sliders paralyzed batters. His 4,875 strikeouts sit second on career strikeouts and his 10.61 strikeouts per nine innings rank first. Johnson was awarded the Cy Young Award five times.

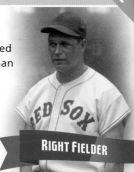

PITCHER

All-Stars Hall of Fame

Fifty first-class players with Hall of Fame potential:

MIKE TROUT *1*
CENTER FIELDER

MOOKIE BETTS *2*
RIGHT FIELDER

CODY BELLINGER *3*
FIRST BASEMAN · OUTFIELDER

JUSTIN VERLANDER *4*
PITCHER

FRANCISCO LINDOR *5*
SHORTSTOP

CHRISTIAN YELICH *6*
OUTFIELDER

GERRIT COLE *7*
PITCHER

JOSÉ RAMÍREZ *8*
THIRD BASEMAN

MAX SCHERZER *9*
PITCHER

ALEX BREGMAN *10*
THIRD BASEMAN · SHORTSTOP

RONALD ACUÑA JR. *11*
OUTFIELDER

NOLAN ARENADO *12*
THIRD BASEMAN

JACOB deGROM *13*
PITCHER

FREDDIE FREEMAN *14*
FIRST BASEMAN

JUAN SOTO *15*
LEFT FIELDER

JOSÉ ALTUVE *16*
SECOND BASEMAN

MATT CHAPMAN *17*
THIRD BASEMAN

AARON JUDGE *18*
RIGHT FIELDER

KRIS BRYANT *19*
OUTFIELDER

CLAYTON KERSHAW *20*
PITCHER

CHRIS SALE *21*
PITCHER

AARON NOLA *22*
PITCHER

PAUL GOLDSCHMIDT *23*
FIRST BASEMAN

JOEY VOTTO *24*
FIRST BASEMAN

J. D. MARTINEZ *25*
OUTFIELDER

These players live and breathe baseball; their hustle and heart set them apart, and they leave nothing on the diamond but priceless moments. Imagine the team you could put together if you had your pick of these players! Who would make the final cut?

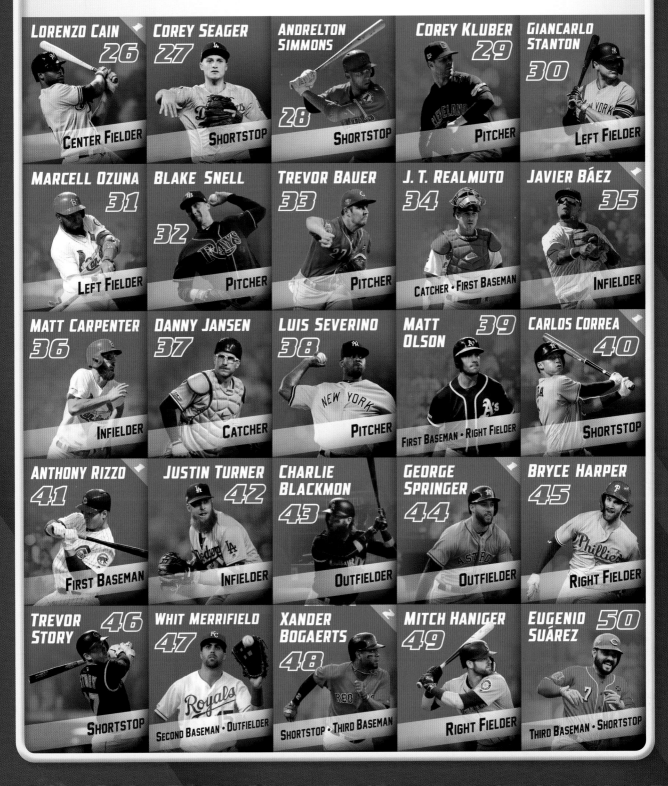

LORENZO CAIN 26 — CENTER FIELDER

COREY SEAGER 27 — SHORTSTOP

ANDRELTON SIMMONS 28 — SHORTSTOP

COREY KLUBER 29 — PITCHER

GIANCARLO STANTON 30 — LEFT FIELDER

MARCELL OZUNA 31 — LEFT FIELDER

BLAKE SNELL 32 — PITCHER

TREVOR BAUER 33 — PITCHER

J. T. REALMUTO 34 — CATCHER · FIRST BASEMAN

JAVIER BÁEZ 35 — INFIELDER

MATT CARPENTER 36 — INFIELDER

DANNY JANSEN 37 — CATCHER

LUIS SEVERINO 38 — PITCHER

MATT OLSON 39 — FIRST BASEMAN · RIGHT FIELDER

CARLOS CORREA 40 — SHORTSTOP

ANTHONY RIZZO 41 — FIRST BASEMAN

JUSTIN TURNER 42 — INFIELDER

CHARLIE BLACKMON 43 — OUTFIELDER

GEORGE SPRINGER 44 — OUTFIELDER

BRYCE HARPER 45 — RIGHT FIELDER

TREVOR STORY 46 — SHORTSTOP

WHIT MERRIFIELD 47 — SECOND BASEMAN · OUTFIELDER

XANDER BOGAERTS 48 — SHORTSTOP · THIRD BASEMAN

MITCH HANIGER 49 — RIGHT FIELDER

EUGENIO SUÁREZ 50 — THIRD BASEMAN · SHORTSTOP

J. D. MARTINEZ — Page 25

FRANCISCO LINDOR — Page 12

BRYCE HARPER — Page 29

AARON JUDGE — Page 21

JACOB deGROM — Page 18

All-Stars
Hall of Fame

STAR PLAYER PROFILES

MARCELL OZUNA — Page 27

GIANCARLO STANTON — Page 26

PAUL GOLDSCHMIDT — Page 23

CHRIS SALE — Page 22

JOSÉ RAMÍREZ — Page 14

MIKE TROUT — Page 10

DANNY JANSEN — Page 28

MOOKIE BETTS — Page 11

MAX SCHERZER — Page 15

FREDDIE FREEMAN — Page 19

Discover more about the person under the baseball cap and the athlete under the jersey: these 20 players are the elite of the elite, but what gives the Mike Trouts, Mookie Bettses, Max Scherzers, and Alex Bregmans their edge?

JOEY VOTTO — Page 24

NOLAN ARENADO — Page 17

CHRISTIAN YELICH — Page 13

ALEX BREGMAN — Page 16

JOSÉ ALTUVE — Page 20

Read on to find out.

MIKE TROUT

All-Stars
Hall of Fame
1

The "Millville Meteor" is currently the MLB's highest-paid player.

Mike is quiet, but his career stats shout that he is a once-in-a-generation player, and a shoo-in for the Hall of Fame. In 2012, his rookie season, Mike became the youngest member of the 30–30 club, and the first in MLB history to hit 30 home runs, steal 45 bases, and earn 125 RBIs in one season. He has Mickey Mantle-like power and speed, plus his game is consistent day in, day out.

PERSONAL DATA

August 7, 1991

Vineland, New Jersey

Right

Right

CAREER HISTORY

LOS ANGELES ANGELS

2011 –

☆ 27 ☆

CAREER HIGHLIGHTS

- Three-time AL MVP and runner-up in every other full season played.
- Eight MLB All-Star and one All-MLB first team selections.
- Seven Silver Slugger and two Hank Aaron awards.

★ ★ ★

CENTER FIELDER

MOOKIE BETTS

You can't teach the sort of skills Mookie has—he's a naturally gifted hitter.

It's no coincidence that Mookie's initials are MLB—baseball is a family passion. Mookie is an all-around skilled ballplayer. In 2018, he must have been wearing his lucky necklace—a plastic bat and ball on a length of string—because he made MLB history, winning MVP, Silver Slugger, and Gold Glove awards, plus a World Series! He also joined the 30–30 club and hit for the cycle.

PERSONAL DATA

October 7, 1992

Nashville, Tennessee

Right

Right

CAREER HISTORY

BOSTON RED SOX
2014 – 2019
★ 50 ★

LOS ANGELES DODGERS
2020 –
★ 50 ★

CAREER HIGHLIGHTS

- First in MLB history to hit 3 homers in 4 games under the age of 26.
- Three Silver Slugger, four Gold Glove, and a Wilson Defensive Player of the Year awards.
- Four All-Star and one All-MLB second team selections.

RIGHT FIELDER

FRANCISCO LINDOR

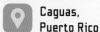

All-Stars
Hall of Fame
5

Every day "Mr. Smile" gets to play is like a dream come true.

Francisco's 2019 season was not a fluke; he's been amazing since the start of his career. With blink-and-you-miss-them hands and great range, this quick-thinking player is always in the right place at the right time, and thanks to his father's coaching—a natural left-hander, he had to clear a bucket of balls right-handed before he could hit left—a switch-hitter from the beginning.

PERSONAL DATA

November 14, 1993

Caguas, Puerto Rico

Switch

Right

CAREER HISTORY

CLEVELAND INDIANS

2015 –

12

CAREER HIGHLIGHTS

- Four-time All-Star and an AL pennant winner.
- Two Gold Glove and two Silver Slugger awards.
- Consecutive winner of Player of the Week followed by AL Player of the Month (2018).

SHORTSTOP

CHRISTIAN YELICH

All-Stars
Hall of Fame
6

Season by season he improved, and in 2018 it all came together.

In high school, Christian was ranked 34th nationally. After two years with the Brew Crew, his stats were out of the park: more than 80 home runs, 200 runs driven in, and 50 stolen bases. He also hit for the cycle twice, 19 days apart, against the same team. "Yeli" hit homers in each of the Brewers' first four games in the 2019 season, making him the sixth player in MLB history—Willie Mays was the first—to achieve this.

PERSONAL DATA

 December 5, 1991

 Thousand Oaks, California

 Left

 Right

OUTFIELDER

CAREER HISTORY

MIAMI MARLINS

2013 – 2017

★ 2 ★

MILWAUKEE BREWERS

2018 –

★ 22 ★

CAREER HIGHLIGHTS

- NL MVP winner and one-time runner-up.
- Three Silver Slugger, two Hank Aaron, and one Gold Glove awards.
- Two All-Star and one All-MLB first team selections.

★ ★ ★

JOSÉ RAMÍREZ

All-Stars Hall of Fame 8

José's hand-eye coordination, plate discipline, and contact skills win out.

José's 2016–2018 seasons were outstanding. He was third in the AL MVP vote two years in a row, and showed he could turn fastballs into home runs at an exceptional rate. A performance slump in late 2018 was followed by a strong opening in 2019, which included hitting his first career grand slam in his first game back after breaking his hand. It's hard to keep a potential Hall of Famer down.

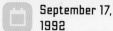

PERSONAL DATA

- September 17, 1992
- Baní, Dominican Republic
- Switch
- Right

CAREER HISTORY

CLEVELAND INDIANS

2013 –

⭐ 11 ⭐

CAREER HIGHLIGHTS

- Two All-Star selections and two Silver Slugger Awards.
- Made the 30–30 club and hit his first career grand slam in 2019.
- 19th player in MLB history to hit more than 56 doubles in one season.

⭐⭐⭐

THIRD BASEMAN

MAX SCHERZER

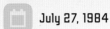
All-Stars
Hall of Fame
9

"Mad Max" is a World Series champ who keeps spitting out power pitches.

In his college days, Max's windup was so violent the whip of his head would send his cap flying. He still puts in a mighty effort, but now it is controlled. Max's fastballs are clocked at 93.8 mph, but last pitches touch 98 mph. His arsenal also includes changeups, curveballs, sliders, and cutters. In 2015, he pitched two no-hitters, and in 2017–2018, two immaculate innings.

PERSONAL DATA

July 27, 1984

Chesterfield, Missouri

Right

Right

CAREER HISTORY

ARIZONA DIAMONDBACKS	DETROIT TIGERS
2008 – 2009	2010 – 2014
★ 39 ★	★ 37 ★

WASHINGTON NATIONALS
2015 –
★ 31 ★

CAREER HIGHLIGHTS

- Seven All-Star and one All-MLB first team selections.
- Three Cy Young Awards and a *Sports Illustrated* Outstanding Pitcher of the Year.
- Career ERA of 3.20 and one of 13 current pitchers with 2,500-plus strikeouts.

PITCHER

ALEX BREGMAN

All-Stars
Hall of Fame
10

Alex demands excellence from himself, and no lead is ever big enough.

When all 30 teams passed on drafting him out of high school in the first round, Alex chose college instead and picked number 30 for his jersey—he knew his worth even then. Commentators talk about his bat speed, strike zone awareness, contact ability, strong arm, plate discipline, and base-running smarts. In 2019, he became the 20th player to hit a grand slam in a World Series.

PERSONAL DATA

March 30, 1994

Albuquerque, New Mexico

Right

Right

CAREER HISTORY

HOUSTON ASTROS

2016 –

★ **2** ★

CAREER HIGHLIGHTS

 First high school player to win USA Baseball Player of the Year Award.

Two All-Star and All-MLB second team selections.

 AL MVP and one-time runner-up, and Silver Slugger Award.

THIRD BASEMAN · SHORTSTOP

NOLAN ARENADO

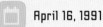

All-Stars
Hall of Fame
12

The third baseman who always performs "magic in the hot corner."

In his less athletic days, his nickname was "Lumbernado." Now it's "Nado," and he mixes consistency with breathtaking acrobatics on the field. Often ranked the league's fifth-most valuable player, Nolan's fielding is beyond compare. In 2015 and 2016, he led the league in home runs and runs batted in. But does Nolan want the fame? No, he just wants to excel.

PERSONAL DATA

April 16, 1991

Newport Beach, California

Right

Right

CAREER HISTORY

COLORADO ROCKIES

2013 –

★ **28** ★

CAREER HIGHLIGHTS

- Five All-Star selections and four Silver Slugger Awards.
- The only infielder to win a Gold Glove in each of his first seven seasons.
- First MLB third baseman to drive in more than 130 runs in three consecutive seasons.

THIRD BASEMAN

JACOB DEGROM

All-Stars
Hall of Fame
13

It's a miracle when a slugger gets a piece of a "deGrominator" pitch.

Sports came easy to this athlete, and his natural ability and long, loose effortless arm action got him to the majors, but hard work keeps him there! He confesses that he only really learned to pitch in 2016. Currently, his fastballs average 96.5 mph, sliders 93.5 mph, and his ERA is 2.43. The long hair went in 2017, but this pitcher has lost none of his power or precision.

PERSONAL DATA

 June 19, 1988

 DeLand, Florida

 Left

 Right

CAREER HISTORY

NEW YORK METS

2014 –

★ 48 ★

CAREER HIGHLIGHTS

- NL Rookie of the Year and Wilson Defensive Player of the Year.
- Two consecutive Cy Young Awards.
- Three All-Star and an All-MLB first team selections.

PITCHER

FREDDIE FREEMAN

All-Stars Hall of Fame 14

A quiet, humble, and friendly player who's become one of baseball's elite.

The only hitters to have better offensive numbers over 4,000 plate appearances are Mike Trout and Paul Goldschmidt. That stat says a lot about Freddie, who has evolved since he was drafted. He's hitting more pitches above 98 mph, and hitting them extremely hard. He's a respected leader at the Braves, and no matter the pitch, this unassuming guy hacks at everything.

PERSONAL DATA

 September 12, 1989

 Fountain Valley, California

 Left

 Right

CAREER HISTORY

ATLANTA BRAVES

2016 –

☆ 5 ☆

CAREER HIGHLIGHTS

- Four All-Star and one All-MLB second team selections.
- Gold Glove and Silver Slugger awards.
- Two-time Wilson Defensive Player of the Year.

FIRST BASEMAN

JOSÉ ALTUVE

All-Stars
Hall of Fame
16

Hits happen when a 66-inch-tall man wields a 33-inch-long bat.

José has a massive strength-to-body-mass ratio. From 2014–2017 he had over 200 hits each season. His best asset is being able to convert a bad pitch into a hit. In the three seasons before he joined the Astros, they had more than 100 losses each season; with José on the team, fortunes were reversed, and the Astros had their first World Series triumph.

PERSONAL DATA

📅 May 6, 1990

📍 Maracay, Venezuela

🏏 Right

⚾ Right

CAREER HISTORY

HOUSTON ASTROS

2011 –

⭐ 27 ⭐

CAREER HIGHLIGHTS

- ⚾ Six All-Star and one All-MLB second team selections.

- ⚾ Five Silver Slugger, and Gold Glove, Lou Gehrig Memorial, and Hank Aaron awards.

- ⚾ AL MVP, *Sports Illustrated* co-Sportsman of the Year, and AP Male Athlete of the Year.

SECOND BASEMAN

AARON JUDGE

All-Stars Hall of Fame 18

All rise for "The Judge"—the tallest and biggest player on the field.

Aaron sets records—and then breaks them. He broke the MLB rookie record for 52 home runs in a rookie season. Some of his other rookie feats put him in the company of Babe Ruth, Lou Gehrig, Joe DiMaggio, and Mickey Mantle. Balls can leave Aaron's bat at 121.1 mph and travel 495 feet. He racked up 100 home runs in the third-fastest time in MLB history.

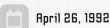

PERSONAL DATA

 April 26, 1992

 Linden, California

 Right

Right

CAREER HISTORY

NEW YORK YANKEES

2016 –

☆ 99 ☆

CAREER HIGHLIGHTS

 AL Rookie of the Year, runner-up AL MVP, and Home Run Derby winner.

 AL Silver Slugger Award and two-time All-Star.

 Wilson Defensive Player of the Year.

★★★

RIGHT FIELDER

CHRIS SALE

All-Stars Hall of Fame 21

This king-of-the-mound power pitcher is almost unhittable.

Chris's strikeout armory is a mid-90 mph fastball, a mid-80 mph changeup, a sinker, and a batter-demoralizing slider. All are equally effective against right-handed or left-handed batters, and his windup is whiplash fast. Only "The Condor" knows the trajectory of his east–west, crossfire delivery. Chris's slider zips this way and that, which is why it is called "The Snitch," after the Quidditch ball in *Harry Potter*.

PERSONAL DATA

- March 30, 1989
- Lakeland, Florida
- Left
- Left

CAREER HISTORY

CHICAGO WHITE SOX
2010 – 2016
★ 49 ★

BOSTON RED SOX
2017 –
★ 41 ★

CAREER HIGHLIGHTS

- Seven All-Star selections and twice AL TSN Pitcher of the Year.
- Two-time leader strikeouts and 2017 MLB career leader in strikeout-to-walk ratio.
- Two immaculate innings and 2,000th strikeout in 1,626 innings pitched (fewest innings in MLB history).

PITCHER

PAUL GOLDSCHMIDT

All-Stars **Hall of Fame** *23*

Paul in a nutshell: consistent, durable, and under the radar.

Paul's greatest asset—and he has many—is his ability to read the pitcher. He spots the tells and reacts with lightning speed. He always gets a jump, whether he's at bat or on base. On top-10 offensive lists, Paul's name is always up there. For a player who shuns the limelight, he doesn't play it safe, and is bold enough to take iffy opportunities and turn them into "Goldy" moments.

PERSONAL DATA

- September 10, 1987
- Wilmington, Delaware
- Right
- Left

CAREER HISTORY

ARIZONA DIAMONDBACKS
2011 - 2018
★ 44 ★

ST. LOUIS CARDINALS
2019 -
★ 46 ★

CAREER HIGHLIGHTS

- Six-time All-Star and two-time runner-up NL MVP.
- Three Gold Glove, four Silver Slugger, and one Hank Aaron awards.
- In the top 10 seven times for fielding percentage at first base.

FIRST BASEMAN

JOEY VOTTO

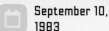

All-Stars
Hall of Fame
24

When playing well, Joey is the Reds' best and purest batter ever.

The best baseball player ever to cross the border from Canada is a perfectionist. In his highlight years—and that's all bar one—he hits, gets on base with more walks than strikeouts, and gets home. Getting out is not on Joey's radar. The same applies to anything distracting: whether training, working out, or prepping for a game, he focuses only on the important stuff, and doesn't sweat the rest.

PERSONAL DATA

September 10, 1983

Toronto, Ontario

Left

Right

CAREER HISTORY

CINCINNATI REDS

2007 –

★ **19** ★

CAREER HIGHLIGHTS

- Six-time All-Star.
- Hank Aaron, Gold Glove, and Lou Gehrig Memorial awards.
- NL MVP and seven-time NL on-base percentage leader.

FIRST BASEMAN

★ ★ ★

J. D. MARTINEZ

All-Stars
Hall of Fame
25

J.D.'s an obsessive student of hitting, and he proves it, game after game.

J.D. started playing baseball at age four, and by middle school he was playing seven times a week and practicing for hours after class. The hard work made him a great slugger, but a 2014 rebuild of his swing turned him into one of the best. J.D.'s batting practice gear might be unusual—there's a Frisbee and basketball—but it must work; J.D. was the 16th-best hitter at the close of 2019.

PERSONAL DATA

August 21, 1987

Miami, Florida

Right

Right

CAREER HISTORY

HOUSTON ASTROS	DETROIT TIGERS
2011 – 2013	2014 – 2017
★ 14 ★	★ 28 ★

ARIZONA DIAMONDBACKS	BOSTON RED SOX
2017	2018 –
★ 28 ★	★ 28 ★

CAREER HIGHLIGHTS

 Three-time All-Star and one-time Hank Aaron Award winner.

 Three Silver Slugger Awards, winning twice in one year at two different positions.

 AL MVP 4th place.

OUTFIELDER

GIANCARLO STANTON

All-Stars
Hall of Fame
30

When he was 20 years old, a Giancarlo minor league home run flew 550 feet.

A month after his colossal minor league home run, Giancarlo was called up to the majors. His first grand slam quickly followed, and long and fast hits kept coming. On the Statcast exit velocity lists, Giancarlo's name appears both frequently and at the top. In 2016, he set an MLB record of 123.9 mph. This big, bad six-foot six-inch slugger is expected to beat his 2016 home-run total of 59.

PERSONAL DATA

- November 8, 1989
- Panorama City, California
- Right
- Right

CAREER HISTORY

FLORIDA/MIAMI MARLINS
2010 – 2017
★ **27** ★

NEW YORK YANKEES
2018 –
★ **27** ★

CAREER HIGHLIGHTS

- Four-time All-Star and one-time NL MVP.
- Silver Slugger, Wilson Defensive Player of the Year, and Hank Aaron awards.
- Home Run Derby winner.

LEFT FIELDER

★ ★ ★

MARCELL OZUNA

All-Stars
Hall of Fame
31

"The Big Bear" is one of the top 25 hitters for quality of contact.

Injuries have resulted in a dip, but Marcell is still in baseball's elite stratosphere. In 2017, he exceeded expectations: he was fourth in batting average and third in home runs. His hit velocity and barrel rate put him in the top 10 percent of the league. In left field, there are few to contest him. Stats are important, but they don't measure the person, and Marcell is also one great guy.

PERSONAL DATA

 November 12, 1990

 Santo Domingo, Dominican Republic

 Right

 Right

LEFT FIELDER

CAREER HISTORY

MIAMI MARLINS	ST. LOUIS CARDINALS
2013 – 2017	2018 – 2019
★ 48 ★	★ 13 ★

ATLANTA BRAVES
2020 –
★ 23 ★

CAREER HIGHLIGHTS

- Two-time All-Star.
- Gold Glove and Silver Slugger awards.
- In 2018, racked up his 100th home run and second grand slam.

DANNY JANSEN

All-Stars Hall of Fame 37

Watch the space on and behind the plate—"Jano's" star is on the rise.

The potential that got this gifted athlete into the majors is evolving gradually into a force to be reckoned with. Danny leads in metrics for catchers, and his game calling is solid. When it comes to the bat, he shuns gloves and has a short, compact swing that is being seasoned with aggression and polish. The biggest change to his game came from an eye test in 2017 and some cool new glasses!

PERSONAL DATA

 April 15, 1995

 Elmhurst, Illinois

 Right

Right

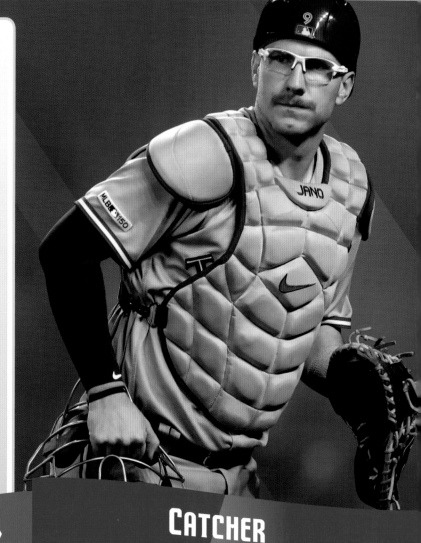

CAREER HISTORY

TORONTO BLUE JAYS

2018 –

☆ **9** ☆

CAREER HIGHLIGHTS

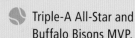

 Triple-A All-Star and Buffalo Bisons MVP.

 Gold Glove finalist.

 All-Star Futures selection.

★ ★ ★

CATCHER

BRYCE HARPER

All-Stars
Hall of Fame
45

The youngest player with 40 homers and 120 walks in a season since Babe Ruth.

Bryce is in good company in the record books. His stats are similar to those of Barry Bonds, and Bryce and Mike Trout both hit their 150th home run at age 24 years, 295 days. Even "Mondo's" swing screams Babe Ruth. When he's in top form, his field and plate game are aggressive and sparks can fly. Bryce has a career OPS of .897 with a 1.109 in 2015. Few other current players can boast similar stats.

PERSONAL DATA

October 16, 1992

Las Vegas, Nevada

Left

Right

CAREER HISTORY

WASHINGTON NATIONALS
2012 – 2018
☆ 34 ☆

PHILADELPHIA PHILLIES
2019 –
☆ 3 ☆

CAREER HIGHLIGHTS

- Golden Spikes and All-Star Futures awards.
- Six-time All-Star and ESPN MLB Person of the Year.
- NL MVP, Hank Aaron, and Silver Slugger awards.

RIGHT FIELDER

PLAYER POSITIONS

There are nine players on the defensive team and their fielding positions are shown in the diagram. The offensive team is the one at bat on home plate.

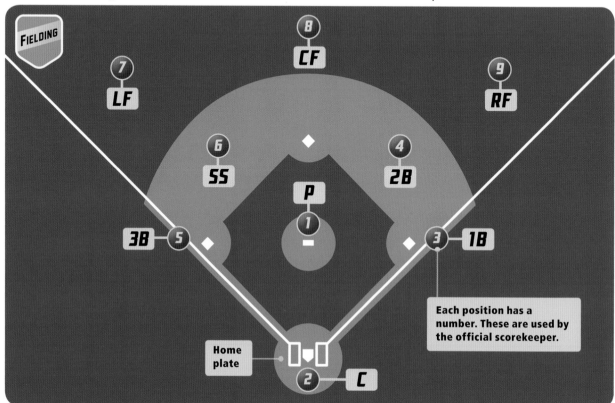

Each position has a number. These are used by the official scorekeeper.

Home plate

Battery

P **Pitcher** throws the ball from the mound to the catcher.

C **Catcher** crouches between hitter and umpire. He receives the ball from the pitcher, calls for pitches using hand signals, and defends the home plate.

Infield

1B **First baseman** fields nearest first base and often throws left-handed.

2B **Second baseman** fields between second and first base and often right-handed with a long-range throw.

3B **Third baseman** defends nearest third base ("hot corner") and requires a strong, accurate, and long throw.

SS **Shortstop** is between second and third base. The shortstop receives more balls than any other defense position.

Outfield

LF **Left fielder** covers the left side of the field. All outfielders need to be fast, accurate throwers, and able to catch balls on the run.

CF **Center fielder** is the "captain" of the outfield and needs pace and a strong throwing arm.

RF **Right fielder** covers the right side of the field and is the team's strongest and most accurate thrower.

FIELDING

Hitter all players on the offensive team are in the batting order.

DH **Designated hitter** this player stands in to bat for the pitcher, and does not play a position in the field.

PH **Pinch hitter** a substitute batter.

PR **Pinch runner** replaces a player on base.

BATTING

GLOSSARY

30–30 club players with 30 home runs and 30 stolen bases in a season.

AL American League.

All-Star (Midsummer Classic) the MLB game between AL and NL All-Stars.

All-Star Futures an MLB game between a team of Minor League prospects from the US and a team of prospects from other countries.

ball a pitch outside of the strike zone where batter does not swing.

changeup a pitch that is 8–15 mph slower than a fastball but retains spin.

curveball forward spin causes the ball to dive as it approaches the plate.

cutter/cut fastball moves toward the pitcher's glove-side hand.

Cy Young Award presented to top pitchers in the MLB.

double where the hitter advances to second base without a fielding mishap or another runner getting out.

earned run average (ERA) how many defense error-free runs a pitcher allowed during an inning.

exit velocity speed of the ball as it comes off the bat.

fastball pitch with backspin that is thrown very hard and fast (over 90 mph).

fielding percentage/average how many times a defensive player handles a battled or thrown ball.

flyball a ball hit high into the air.

Gold Glove Award presented to top MLB fielders in each position.

Golden Spikes Award presented to top US amateur baseball player.

grand slam a home run hit with runners on all three bases, scoring four runs.

ground ball batted ball that bounces and rolls before being fielded.

Hank Aaron Award honors the top hitters in the MLB.

hit for the cycle a batter getting a single, double, triple, and home run in the same game.

home run (HR) when a batter hits a fair ball and scores on the play without being putout or without the benefit of an error.

Home Run Derby contest between the best AL and NL home run hitters to hit the most home runs in four minutes.

immaculate inning when a pitcher strikes out all three batters he faces in one inning with three pitches each.

Lou Gehrig Memorial Award MLB player displaying character and integrity.

majors abbreviated reference to MLB.

MLB Major League Baseball consisting of 15 AL and 15 NL teams.

MVP Most Valuable Player.

NL National League.

no hitter a nine-innings game and a single pitcher where the offense does not record a hit.

on-base percentage (OBP) how often a batter reaches base.

on-base plus slugging (OPS) how often a hitter gets on base and hits for power.

perfect game a nine-inning game where no batter reaches a base.

rookie player with less than 130 at-bats or 50 innings pitched in the majors or less than 45 days on active roster in the MLB.

runs driven in (RBI) runs scored during a batter's appearance at the plate.

Silver Slugger Award presented to the best offensive player at each position in the MLB.

sinker a type of fastball with down and sideways movement.

slider like the curveball but faster, with movement away from pitcher's arm-side.

slugging percentage (SLG) total number of bases a player records at-bat. Excludes walks and hit-by-pitches.

steal (stolen base) occurs when a base runner advances by taking a base he isn't entitled to.

strike when a batter swings and misses, does not swing in the strike zone, or hits an uncaught foul ball.

strike zone area over home plate from midpoint between a batter's shoulders and the top of the uniform pants and a point just below the kneecap.

strikeout when a batter gets three strikes at bat, and is usually called out.

strikeouts-to-walks the number of strikeouts a pitcher records for each walk he allows.

switch-hitter batter who regularly bats both right- and left-handed.

Triple-A All-Star annual professional Minor League game.

walk (base on balls) after four pitches ruled as balls by the umpire, the hitter can move to first base.

Wilson Defensive Player of the Year top MLB defensive player in each position.

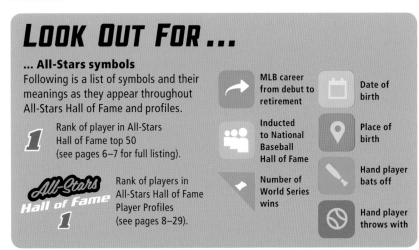

LOOK OUT FOR...

... All-Stars symbols
Following is a list of symbols and their meanings as they appear throughout All-Stars Hall of Fame and profiles.

1 Rank of player in All-Stars Hall of Fame top 50 (see pages 6–7 for full listing).

All-Stars Hall of Fame 1 Rank of players in All-Stars Hall of Fame Player Profiles (see pages 8–29).

MLB career from debut to retirement

Inducted to National Baseball Hall of Fame

Number of World Series wins

Date of birth

Place of birth

Hand player bats off

Hand player throws with

INDEX